Out There?

MYSTERIOUS URBAN MYTHS

John Townsend

Raintree

Chicago, Illinois

For information, address the publisher:
Raintree, 100 N. LaSalle, Suite 1200, Chicago, IL 60602

Printed and bound in China
08 07 06 05 04
10 9 8 7 6 5 4 3 2 1

Library of Congress Cataloging-in-Publication Data
Townsend, John, 1955-
  Mysterious urban myths / John Townsend.
     v. cm. -- (Out there?)
Includes bibliographical references and index.
Contents: Crime -- Animals -- Medical myths -- Scary tales -- Mistakes
-- Dead ends -- Mix and match.
  ISBN 1-4109-0567-5
  1. Urban folklore. 2. Legends. [1. Urban folklore. 2. Folklore.] I.
Title.
  GR78.T69 2004
  398.2'091732--dc21
                        2003010546

Acknowledgments
The publisher wishes to thank the following for permission to reproduce photographs.
Pp. 4–5 Fortean Picture Library; pp. 5 (bottom), 9, 20–21, 36, 46–47, 50 Photodisc; pp. 5 (middle), 28 Touhig Sion/Corbis; p. 5 (top), 6–7, 7, 8, 12–13, 24, 27, 29, 30–31, 32–33, 33, 36–37, 38, 42–43, 44, 45, 48–49 Tudor Photography; p. 6 Charles Gupton/Corbis; pp. 8–9 Topham Picturepoint; p. 10, 10–11 Stockbyte; p. 11 Tim Page/Corbis; p. 12 Kim Sayer/Corbis; p. 13 Albey Towers; pp. 14–15 Don Mason/Corbis; pp. 15, 20 Gerard Lacz/NHPA; p. 16 Digital Vision; pp. 16–17 Hans and Judy Beste/Ardea; p. 17 Steve Bloom; p. 18 Trevor McDonald/NHPA; pp. 18–19 Martin Harvey/NHPA; p. 19 Nik Wheeler/Corbis; p. 21 Manfred Danegger/NHPA; p. 22 Ed Young/Corbis; pp. 22–23 Phil Schermeister/Corbis; p. 23 ER Productions/Corbis; pp. 24–25 Alan Goldsmith/Corbis; p. 24 A. Weaving/Ardea; p. 26 Claude Nuridsany and Marie Perrennou/Science Photo Library; pp. 26–27 John Walmsley; pp. 28–29 Rex Features; p. 30 John Birdsall Photography; p. 31 Corbis; pp. 34–36 Strauss/Curtis/Corbis; p. 37 Snopes.com; pp. 38–39 James A. Sugar/Corbis; p. 39 Stephen Dalton/NHPA; p. 40 Alamy Images; p. 41 Richard T. Nowitz/Corbis; p. 41 Steve Starr/Corbis; p. 42 Alamy Images; pp. 43, 46 Bob Krist/Corbis; p. 47 James Carmichael Jr./NHPA; p. 49 Pictorial Press.
Cover photographer of used with permission of Thomas Lang/Corbis.

Every effort has been made to contact copyright holders of any material reproduced in this book. Any omissions will be rectified in subsequent printings if notice is given to the publishers. All the Internet addresses (URLs) given in this book were valid at the time of going to press. However, due to the dynamic nature of the Internet, some addresses may have changed, or sites may have changed or ceased to exist since publication. While the author and publishers regret any inconvenience this may cause readers, no responsibility for any such changes can be accepted by either the author or the publishers.

CONTENTS

Some words are shown in bold, **like this.** You can find out what they mean by looking in the glossary. You can also look out for them in the "Weird Words" box at the bottom of most pages.

MYSTERIOUS TALES

TRUE OR FALSE?

The urban myths in this book are given a code:

- **T** = TRUE
  It is thought the story is based on real details.

- **F** = FALSE
  It seems the whole story is made up.

- **?** = Who knows?
  It is hard to tell how much of the story is made up.

Whether they are true or not, the stories are still worth telling.

Are urban myths just modern fairy tales for adults? **>>**

You can never tell. That is the mystery with **myths.** How much is really true? How much gets added each time the story is told?

absurd   crazy or ridiculous
myth   made-up tale, told over the years and passed on

THE MYSTERY OF URBAN MYTHS

Urban myths are told over and over again. Many were based on true events to begin with, but often they are hard to believe. Many have mysterious endings. But the real mystery is in figuring out which stories have been made up.

ANY TIME, ANY PLACE

Urban myths are stories of our time. They could be told in any town around the world. They often begin with the words, "You may not believe this but my friend's friend met someone who this really happened to . . . ."

TELLING TALES

An urban myth works best when people believe it really happened to someone they know. Some urban myths have a message or a warning. Some have a spooky ring of truth. Many are funny, and a few are scary. Most have more than a hint of the weird, **absurd,** or the disgusting. There is often a twist at the end of these tales.

COMING SOON

New urban myths are being told all the time. Just where and how do they start? New tales of mystery are about to unfold.

FIND OUT LATER . . .

Just how mysterious was the note left on a car?

Should we believe the story of the killer cactus?

Can we explain what the dog had in its throat?

urban myth modern popular story that could be true but is probably not

CRIME

The goofy mistakes of failed crooks make good stories. Sometimes it is hard to believe that people can really be so stupid . . . .

THE CROOK WHO USED HER HEAD

On a hot day, a woman walked out of the supermarket and fainted. It must have been from the heat, because she was wearing a fur coat and hat. A doctor ran over to cool her down, thinking she had heatstroke. He undid her thick coat and took off her hat. Now he could see what was wrong. Inside her coat was a frozen turkey, and under her hat was a bag of frozen shrimp. She was a shoplifter. She had chilled her blood, numbed her brain, and gotten frostbite. **?**

"You will never believe this, but I just heard that a man on our street was arrested . . . ."

DID YOU KNOW?

- **Urban myths** are sometimes called urban **legends.**

- They are stories that people like to believe are true, but they cannot be proven.

- People usually tell urban myths about a friend of a friend.

cashier   person who works at a cash register or a bank
legend story based on a grain of truth

HIGH-TECH LIE DETECTOR

The police had caught a robber, but he would not admit to his crime. So the police tried a trick. They told him they were about to use a new **lie detector.** They got a pan from the kitchen and put it on his head. Wires went from the handle to the photocopier.

"Did you rob the store?" they asked.

"No," he said.

The police pressed the copy button and paper came out of the photocopier. The word "lie" was printed on the paper. The robber gave up. "Okay, you win. The machine knows the truth. I did it."

The police got their man.

A nice story—but doubtful! (?)

Found out—by a simple trick! **<<**

A crook with more than just a price on his head. **>>**

SAME TRICK—MESSY END

Another story tells of a shoplifter with a bald head. He hid a frozen steak under his cap. By the time he got to the checkout, it was thawing. Blood was dripping down his face. The **cashier** screamed. They took him to the emergency room and then arrested him!

lie detector machine that records a person's reactions during questioning

CALL THE COPS!

Burglars broke into a house, and one of them used the phone to call a friend. He was wearing gloves so he would not leave any fingerprints, but this made him press the wrong button. Instead of 411 he called 911. The police traced the call and arrested the crooks. **T**

FOOLED

Even if all the details in these **urban myths** are not exactly true, the police deal with goings-on like this most weekends.

THE CHAINSAW MADMAN

A woman answered her door late one night and screamed at what she saw. She slammed the door and ran to call the police. A man dressed in a hockey mask stood on her doorstep, waving a roaring chainsaw. She hid upstairs, fearing she was about to be the next victim of the chainsaw-madman.

Police raced to her house, but when they arrived, the chainsaw-madman had gone. The woman was a **nervous** wreck. Police began to search the area.

Dialing with gloves on was a bad idea for the crook who called the police by mistake! **‹‹**

WEIRD WORDS awkward   embarrassed and unsure of oneself
intruder   someone who breaks into another person's property

WRONG ADDRESS

Police found the **sinister** figure at the door of another house. They grabbed him at gunpoint, threw his chainsaw to the ground, and stretched him out on the lawn. The front door opened, and inside there was a costume party in full swing. The man the police had arrested was a guest. He had dressed up as the rap star Eminem and wanted to burst into the party with style.

The police said later, "It turned out that the man had visited the wrong door earlier. He scared the woman out of her wits, so he ran off feeling very **awkward**." ?

This costume was too realistic!

IT COULD HAPPEN . . .

In 1992 a sixteen-year-old student from Japan was in Louisiana. The student was asked to a Halloween party. He did not know the area and rang the wrong doorbell, wearing his scary costume. He was shot dead when the homeowner mistook him for an **intruder**. Ⓣ

sinister   appearing to be harmful or evil
urban myth   modern popular story that could be true

SURPRISE, SURPRISE

A woman found a dead cat by her parked car. She decided to take it home and bury it, so she put it in her shopping bag. Just then a thief zoomed by on a motorcycle and snatched the bag. When he looked inside, he swerved off the road and crashed. **?**

KEEPING A CLOSE WATCH

A man had just caught a train when he saw that his watch was missing. As the train began to move, he turned to see a boy on the platform who was waving and tapping his wrist, saying, "Just in time." Thinking the boy had stolen his watch, the man reached out of the train and grabbed the boy's collar, only to rip it off as the train moved away. He called his wife on his cell phone to tell her what had happened. Before he could speak, she said, "I've been trying to get hold of you. Did you know you left your watch behind on the table this morning?" **?**

cashier   someone who works at a cash register or a bank

HOLD UP

A delivery boy was paid by a friend to take a message and a bag to the bank. He sped off on his motorcycle and parked outside the bank. When he went inside, he handed the envelope to the **cashier,** as he had been told. Suddenly the alarms went off. Guards rushed around him as he stood calmly in his leather outfit and crash helmet. The guards pointed guns at his head and yelled, "Freeze!"

Later at the police station, they showed him the note that was inside the envelope:

> Fill the bag with money. I've got a gun. I'm not afraid to use it. No funny stuff.

The only funny stuff was his friend's idea of a joke.

Better than a night on the street?

Not every bag is what it seems . . . .

11

THE MESSAGE

The owner of a sports car kept alarms, chains, and locks on it to make sure it was safe. Now he could sleep at night. One morning his car was still chained, but it had been turned around. A note under the wiper blade read: "If we want this car, we'll take it."

(F)

No car is safe from a determined thief.

CAR TROUBLE

Cars are in many **urban myths**. These **tall tales** about cars and their owners tell of events on the wrong side of the law.

TAKEN FOR A RIDE

A family lived in the wealthy part of town. One of their cars in the driveway was a sports car. They always left the keys inside this car. One morning it was missing, and no one knew where it was. A few hours later the car was back in the driveway with a note. It said:

Dear Neighbors, please forgive us. We live nearby and had a family emergency.

We had to borrow your car without asking. Please accept these tickets as thanks.

culprit   guilty person

A KIND THOUGHT

Pinned to the note were theater tickets for the whole family to attend a performance the next week.

"How kind," they thought. "What friendly neighbors. They've even cleaned the car for us."

The next week they all went to the theater with their free tickets. When they returned home, they found another note on the front door. It said: "Hope you enjoyed the show. We missed the sports car!"

As the family went indoors, they found the lights did not work. There were no light bulbs. In fact, the whole house was empty. They looked around in horror in the dark. Everything they owned had been stolen. Ⓕ

GOOD NEWS AND BAD NEWS

A woman came back to her parked car and found it had been dented. Then she saw a note on the windshield and thought the **culprit** had left his details:

I've just smashed up your car. A crowd is watching me. Good news: I'm writing this to look like I'm leaving my name. Bad news: I'm not!

⁇ It seems likely that the dented car story has happened. ❮❮

tall tale   story that is very silly and hard to believe

ANIMALS

AN OLD STORY WITH MANY TWISTS

The "sick dog" myth goes back at least 60 years:

- Sometimes the pet is a cat.
- Sometimes the food is salmon, mushrooms, or cold meat.
- Sometimes the pet has been killed by a car.

But the poor guests always end up at the hospital!

Urban **myths** about pets are often funny because we never quite understand animals.

THE SICK DOG

A woman was preparing for an important dinner party. Her husband's new boss was coming, so she spent all morning cooking fresh shrimp. The dog ate one, so she put him outside just as the guests arrived. After they had eaten the shrimp, a neighbor called and said, "Your dog looks very ill." The woman was afraid that the shrimp had poisoned the dog, so she took all the guests to the hospital to get their stomachs pumped. When she got home, another neighbor asked, "Is your dog all right? I'm afraid I dropped a brick on his head." (?)

Poisoned, bashed on the head, or playing dead?

horrified   shocked and disgusted or fearful

WHOSE DOG?

A girl wanted to get on the good side of her old, rich aunt. They had not met for years, so the girl visited her at home. As she was ringing the doorbell, a little dog came yapping at her feet. It followed her into the large house. The girl talked with her aunt in a very nice room, with the dog jumping on the fine furniture, sniffing the cookies, and getting mud all over the carpet. The girl thought it was a disgusting dog, but she thought she had better be kind about it. "What a lovely little dog you have, Auntie."

Her aunt looked **horrified.** "I thought the awful thing was yours!" ⑦

ANIMAL MYTHS

- A swan can break your leg with its wing if you get near.
- Bats like to get tangled in your hair.
- If you hold a dog's lower jaw, it cannot bite you.

A popular animal **myth** is that parrots find swear words easier to learn. Perhaps it depends on their owner! ❮❮

---

myth made-up tale, told over time

RHINO RUMP

A superglue salesman was showing a party of Russian customers around his city. He took them to the zoo and said, "Our superglue is so strong I could stick my hands to that rhino."

The man put a few drops on his hands and placed them on the rhino's rear end. They stuck tight, but the rhino did not like it. It ran around its pen, with the salesman dragging behind. The angry rhino had to be drugged before the man's hands could be released.

The Russians bought three crates of the glue. **F**

Some people will go to any lengths to sell something.

What has this snake eaten to cause such a large bulge?

Rhinoceros is not just the name given to a large, thick-skinned animal with a horn. There is also a rhinoceros beetle. For its size, this beetle is one of the world's strongest animals. It can carry 850 times its own weight. That is like a person being able to carry ten elephants. **T**

SWALLOWED BY A SNAKE

Three boys were recently camping in the jungle in South America. In the middle of the night, one boy woke up to feel something sliding over his leg. He sat up to tell the others, but only one friend was there. They shone a flashlight outside the tent, only to see a huge snake moving away from the tent. It was so fat it could hardly move. They grabbed hold of it and managed to cut it open. Their friend was inside and still alive. Ⓕ

This particular **myth** is not true, but it could happen. A giant boa constrictor can swallow a deer whole. A child would be a snake snack.

A boa squeezes its **prey** to death before swallowing it whole. ⌄⌄

IT COULD HAPPEN

It has been known for people to be eaten by large snakes.

In 1972 a python took a fourteen-year-old boy from a **rice paddy** in Burma. Local people caught the snake and cut out the victim's body. They cooked and ate the snake.

rice paddy   flooded field in which rice is grown

SNAPPY SALTIE

A tourist in northern Australia wanted to take a photo of a saltwater crocodile at a lake. He snapped a picture—but the croc took a snap back. It bit off his arm. When the lab developed his photo, two workers fainted and one threw up.
Ⓕ

Imagine finding this beast in your bathroom! ≫

THE SEWERS OF NEW YORK

Our fear of large **reptiles** has brought about many **urban myths.** For years people have told stories of huge alligators living in the sewers of large cities. They grow fat on rats and all the waste.

WHERE DO THEY COME FROM?

There is a big **trade** in baby alligators. People think they are cute pets to keep in fish tanks. But the alligators grow too big. Finally people flush them down the toilet. In the sewers, they make a nest below the city and breed down there. Some sewer workers have gone down to repair drains and have never been seen again.   Ⓕ

reptiles   group of cold-blooded animals
survive   to stay alive despite dangers

CROCODILE TEARS?

A young man moved into a basement apartment in New York City. One night he was sitting on the toilet, when he felt a terrible pain in his left buttock. He leapt up to find a small alligator hanging from his behind. The animal had squeezed up through the drains in its search for fresh meat.

When the man went to the hospital to have stitches, the doctor said this was now a common injury. Alligator teeth often chew human behinds! (F)

NO NEED TO WORRY

Alligators **thrive** in sunny Florida. But it is hard to believe they could **survive** in the New York sewer system, where the winters can be very cold.

GOLFING HANDICAP

On a golf course in Palm Beach, Florida, an alligator lay in wait in a pond by the fifth green. A golfer went ahead of his friends to find his ball. He was never seen again. The police supposedly opened up the alligator and found the golfer inside. (F)

Some golf courses are more challenging than others.

thrive   to grow in strength and health
trade   buying and selling of goods

Eagles do not normally swoop down and carry off small dogs. Some may attack a dog on the ground, and some may even briefly lift one up in the air, but it is rare for an eagle to make off with a dog. Then again, it is possible.

Another reason to keep small dogs on leashes.

BIRD ATTACKS

Myths about bird attacks are **far-fetched**—but some eagles are very big. Perhaps every so often there could be truth in some **rumors** . . . .

VALDEZ, ALASKA

A woman in Alaska screamed as a bald eagle flew down and snatched her small dog up into the air. The pet was in the front yard when the eagle swooped down from a tree. Before the woman could act, the eagle flew off, with the yapping dog grabbed in its **talons.** **?**

MAINE

A great horned owl was said to have taken off with a 22 pound (10 kilogram) **Pekingese** dog. The owl then went after a cat and an old woman. This myth has not been proven. **F**

far-fetched   sounding too strange to be true
Pekingese   breed of small dog with long hair and a snub nose

FLYING HIGH

In 1932 a four-year-old was playing in her yard in Leka in northern Norway. Suddenly a huge sea eagle dived out of the sky. Its wingspan was 8 feet (2.5 meters). Its talons dug into her arms as it rose up in the air and flew up to a cliff a mile away. Finally, the eagle dropped the girl on a ledge. She screamed and her parents found her. She was fine. They kept her dress with the holes from the talons as proof. Her name is Svanhild Hansen. Hard to believe, but this story is true. Ⓣ

UP, UP, AND AWAY

If eagle owls can carry off big rabbits, small dogs could easily be on the menu. In February 2000 a small dog was scooped up by an eagle owl in Great Britain. The dog escaped and got back home. He was scratched, but he got over his first flight. Ⓣ

Beware: eagle owls are stronger than they look. ❯❯

MEDICAL MYTHS

Hospitals are full of weird stories. Along with the pain, there is often a funny side. Medical **myths** can certainly make us smile.

THE FARMER'S HAND

A farmer had an accident in his combine harvester and cut off his hand. He picked up the hand, drove to the local store, and packed it in frozen peas. Later, he parked at the emergency room and got doctors to sew his hand back on.

There are true reports similar to this. ?

Rachel will never forget her summer job! >>

NURSING HOME

Rachel was glad to get a summer vacation job. It was in a nursing home. One elderly woman said she felt ill, and as night fell, she got worse. They sent for the doctor. The priest came and gave the **last rites,** just in time. It was too late for the doctor now.

It was Rachel's job to lay out the body. She washed the woman's body and got her ready for the **undertaker.** She brushed her hair and folded her hands over her chest.

evidence   information to help prove if something is true
last respects   final farewell to someone who has died

LAST RESPECTS

The woman's family came to pay their **last respects.** They all sat around the bed in silence. The only sound was the slow ticking of the clock. Suddenly, there was a noise and someone screamed.

HAPPY ENDING

Everyone looked up. The old lady was sitting up with a smile. "Oh, I'd love a cup of tea," she said. They could not believe it.

The strange thing was, the woman had done the very same thing the year before. All her family could do was tear up the plans they had made for the funeral and make some tea! **T**

Could this really happen? You bet. This one is true.

THE FALSE LEG

Two thugs came across an old er man who was limping. One thug kicked him, and the old man's false leg flew up in the air. The leg fell back to earth, kicking the thug in the mouth and knocking him flat.

It is a good story but, like the leg, it is false. **F**

Would the **evidence** stand up in court? 〉〉

TRAVEL BUG

A student went backpacking around Europe. When she came back, she found a red mark on her hand. She put cream on it, but her skin was really itchy. One day she gave it a hard scratch. The skin burst and out popped hundreds of baby spiders.

NASTY INSIDES

There are not many things more disgusting than the thought of living things getting inside our bodies. **Urban myths thrive** on such **grisly** ideas.

SPROUTS

A schoolboy in the United Kingdom had a close call. One evening his mother told him to wipe his nose, since he had something green poking out of one nostril. He could not get rid of it, so his mother took a closer look and saw a small leaf sticking out of his nose. She gave it a tug and began to pull out a tomato plant. It was growing inside his nose. It was firmly attached and just would not come out.

Another good reason not to scratch bites.

grisly   causing horror and disgust

BRAIN FOOD

A few months before, the boy had sneezed while eating a tomato. One of the tomato seeds must have shot up his nose and gotten stuck. And that is where it began to sprout— where it was dark, warm, and wet.

The boy was rushed to the hospital, where doctors had to operate. It was very serious. In just a few more days, the roots would have damaged his brain. They removed the plant whole, put it in a little pot, and let him take it home to grow in the garden.

These are well-known myths. They are great tales but not true.

BAD HAIR DAY

A schoolgirl had very long hair. She kept it piled up on her head and did not wash it. In a math class there was a clicking noise, and her hair started moving. At first it seemed to be lice. But the school nurse found a nest in her hair—alive with cockroaches.

ONE IN THE EYE

Before a woman boarded the plane home from Africa, she got dust in her eye. During the flight, her eye became so sore she needed medical help when she got to the airport. Imagine her horror when the doctor removed a freshly hatched **maggot** from under her eyelid. Ⓕ

Perhaps the cleaners are the most dangerous things in a hospital! ❱❱

SWITCHED OFF

One hospital had a real mystery. On Fridays there were always more deaths in one of the **wards.** The mystery was solved after a few months. A doctor just happened to be walking past when a cleaner was at work. She polished the floor in the intensive care ward each Friday. The doctor watched in horror as she went to the socket on the wall to plug in her floor polisher. She pulled out the plug that was already in the socket—and unplugged three patients' life-support systems!

This story has become a bit of a classic. But do not worry—it is totally untrue. Ⓕ

embarrass   make to feel awkward and ashamed
maggot   worm-like, young stage of a fly

STUCK

Doctors tell many stories about people who get stuck in **embarrassing** places.

One winter a woman got her lips stuck to her car door. She could not call for help and waited hours for someone to get a doctor. She had tried to **defrost** the lock by blowing on it. Her lips had frozen to the metal door. ?

STUCK FAST

A man got stuck in a toilet seat in a train. As the train gained speed, it sucked him down even tighter. When the train shot into a tunnel, the **suction** suddenly reversed. He shot off the seat, and his head got stuck in the towel holder. Doctors had to free him. F

MEDICAL BLUNDERS

- In Britain a patient got sick after a daffodil somehow got into his hospital dinner.
- In Holland a student doctor was fired after roaring through the **ward** on a motorcycle.
- A patient's behind caught fire when a spark ignited medical alcohol on the operating table.

T All are true.

Hospital food can be really strange.

suction   gripping from the removal of air, causing a vacuum
ward   section of a hospital for certain kinds of patients

SCARY TALES

STILL ALIVE

A woman went to the butcher to get some cheap meat for her dog. The butcher found her a cow's heart. When she got home, she unwrapped the meat to put on a plate, but it moved. The heart was beating, and it jumped from her hands. Ⓕ

People have always loved stories that send shivers down their backs. **Urban myths** have their fair share of tales that scare.

OUT IN THE BUSH

A woman was driving home late one night in her four-wheel-drive jeep. It was on a **remote** road in the **outback** in Australia, where robbers often struck. Ahead of her she saw a car parked across the middle of the narrow road. It was not wise to slow down, so she pushed her foot down on the accelerator pedal. She roared off the road and over the bumpy **scrub**. The jeep bumped along, then turned back onto the road past the car.

ambush   to attack by surprise
outback   wild country in Australia, miles away from towns

THE NEXT DAY

When the woman got home, she called the police to tell them about the mysterious vehicle.

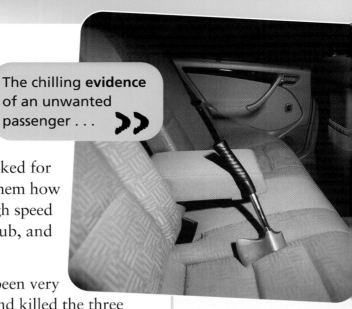

The chilling **evidence** of an unwanted passenger . . . ▶▶

In the morning, the police asked for more information. She told them how she had driven her jeep at high speed off the road, through the scrub, and then back onto the road.

The police told her she had been very lucky. She had driven over and killed the three armed men who were waiting to **ambush** her. They had been killers with a price on their heads. Now all they had were tire marks on their heads.

Maybe most people want this **myth** to be true. Sadly, it is just made up! Ⓕ

Driving along a deadly quiet road is enough to scare anyone. ◀◀

THE PASSENGER

A woman was driving along a road late one night. A car behind flashed its lights, overtook her, and pulled up. The driver ran toward the woman's car just as someone jumped out of her back door. "Did you know," the man said, "there was someone in your backseat with an ax?" Ⓕ

remote   far-away place in the middle of nowhere
scrub   thorny bushes and tufts of grass

MYSTERY MYTHS

Many scary **urban myths** have the same ideas.

- A dangerous **intruder** has broken in.
- He is still in the room or somewhere in the house.
- A lone female is unaware of what **lurks** just a few feet away.

These scary **myths** are often told late at night. Even though they are not true, **nervous** people may feel a shudder . . . .

LATE NIGHT STUDENT

Two girls shared a room at college. One was studying late in the library and went back to their room to get her notes. She left the light off so she would not **disturb** her roommate. She felt around the desk, got her papers, and left. Much later she went back to the room, and this time she turned on the light. Her roommate had been murdered. There was writing in lipstick on the mirror: "Aren't you glad you didn't turn on the light?" Ⓕ

This creepy message has made the late-night student myth a favorite. ◄◄

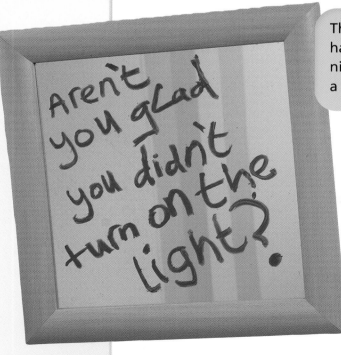

30   **WEIRD WORDS**

disturb   to interrupt someone's rest
lurk   to wait around, ready to strike

THE BABYSITTER

A girl was babysitting late at night in a large, old house. She was alone in charge of a sleeping baby. The phone rang, so she picked it up. There was a scary voice on the other end that told her she was going to be strangled. The calls came every five minutes. She felt very scared and reported the calls to the phone company. Then the phone rang again. This time it was the telephone operator. The news was chilling. "Get out quickly. Those calls are coming from the other phone in the house."

But we should not be too scared. It is just a myth—we think.

The dog in this myth is always a Rottweiler.

The story of a babysitter getting scary phone calls has been used in horror movies.

AN OLD FAVORITE

A woman arrived home to find her dog choking. She took the dog to the vet and left it overnight. Later the vet called in panic. He told her to get out of the house quickly. Human fingers were stuck in the dog's throat. The injured intruder could still be in the house. ?

nervous easily scared

NEARLY DEAD

Myths like this one are well known. They are just right for telling in the dark.

A woman was at a bar by herself when a stranger began to talk to her. They both got along well, and she did not notice when he slipped powder into her drink.

THE NEXT MORNING

The woman opened her eyes. She was freezing and felt a pain in her back. She was lying in a bathtub in a hotel room. It was full of ice. As she sat up, she saw a note. It said:

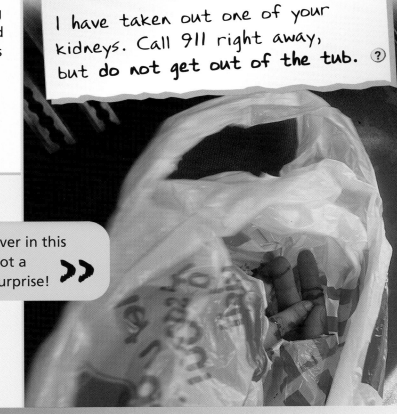

I have taken out one of your kidneys. Call 911 right away, but do not get out of the tub. (?)

SCARY HAND

Bus drivers find all sorts of things left behind on the seats in their buses. People do not just leave behind bags or gloves. Not long ago, a driver found a plastic bag on his bus. When he looked inside the bag, he saw a human hand. (?)

The driver in this myth got a nasty surprise! >>

cleaver   knife with a heavy, wide blade
vanish   to disappear

THE HITCHHIKER

A man was driving along a country road late at night. Suddenly, he saw a girl hitchhiker in his lights, so he stopped the car. "You'd better get in," he said. "It's a cold night to be out walking." She smiled and got into the car.

Soon they came to a small town. "I live here," she said, pointing to a house. The man stopped the car and let her out, but she just **vanished**. He went to the house to see if she had gone inside. A woman opened the door and said his mysterious passenger was her daughter who had died on the road that very night the year before. Ⓕ

HAIRY HAND

A man stopped his car to give an old woman a ride. After a few miles, the old woman's coat and scarf slipped. The driver saw a hairy hand gripping a handbag with a meat **cleaver** sticking out of it. It was covered in fresh blood. Ⓕ

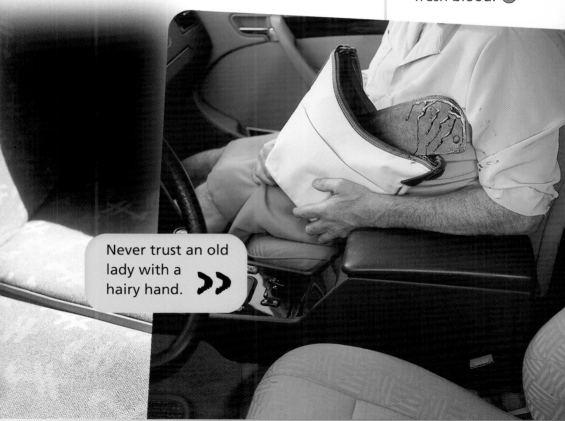

Never trust an old lady with a hairy hand. ❯❯

MISTAKES

Why are many urban myths funny?

Maybe it is because they could happen to any of us. People can be:
■ unlucky;
■ just plain stupid;
■ caught by surprise.

We can laugh because we do not know the people involved, or even if the events really happened.

There is nothing like other people's **blunders** to make good **urban myths**.

OOPS

A man and his wife decided to go to the store in their car. But the car would not start. "I'll stay and fix it. You go on the bus," the man said.

When his wife came home, the car was still in the driveway. Legs were sticking out underneath. She gave one leg a quick squeeze and said, "Hi, sweetie." But when she went indoors, her husband was in the kitchen. They rushed outside to find the man from the local garage still lying under the car. He had knocked himself out when he bashed his head in surprise. (?)

It is hard to tell a person by their legs. And **embarrassing** if you get it wrong. >>

OOPS AGAIN!

Two college students went on vacation and decided to stay an extra day. It meant they missed a math exam. They were not worried because they planned to tell the professor they were late getting back because of a flat tire. How could he possibly know they were lying?

TOUGH QUESTION

When the students got back to college, they told the professor their story and asked if they could take the exam another time. He agreed, but said that they had to take the exam in separate rooms. They did this and both found the exam very easy. But then they read the last question, worth 95 percent of the total grade. It was a very short question with only four words: "Which tire was flat?" ?

UNHAPPY CAT

Many new urban myths spread quickly on the Internet. A fake photo can look very real. A woman took her cat to have its fur trimmed. She asked for a line cut, which is just a trim. They thought she said "a lion cut."

> This hair looks good on a lion, but on a little house cat? >>

HI-TECH MISTAKES

Whether it is cell phones cooking your brain cells or the television remote control setting off the neighbor's car alarm—we live in an age where **gadgets** can go wrong. Modern **technology** is behind many **urban myths.**

MICROWAVE TROUBLE

A busy hotel kitchen bought a new top-of-the-line microwave oven. There was a good place for it in the kitchen on a low shelf at waist height. The chef was pleased with his new gadget. He could reheat many dishes in it at the same time. It was extra large and had a "super-strength" button. The first time he used this button was also his last.

GADGET MYTHS

- **Pacemakers** can cause heart attacks when the wearer goes through airport security screens.
- A virus attacks all computers every Friday the 13th, unless you have special software.
- Cell phones can cause explosions at gas stations and on oil rigs.

Believe these and you will believe anything. **F**

What is the chef's special tonight?

WEIRD WORDS

gadget small electronic or mechanical device
pacemaker electronic device to help steady the heartbeat

COOKED TO A SIZZLE

A customer asked for some piping hot chili. This was just the job for the new microwave on "super-strength." The chef pressed the button and turned his back on the microwave. As he beat some eggs, he was shocked to see them steam and bubble. His insides were doing the same thing. He soon fell dead on the floor.

The microwave door did not seal correctly, and microwaves leaked out. They not only cooked the chili, but they cooked the chef's insides to a crisp.

A true story? No, it is false. Even so, some people never trust microwave ovens. **F**

INTERNET TOILETS

There was a **rumor** on the Internet that Microsoft had invented the iLoo. It was a portable bathroom in which people could also use the Internet. A businessman was supposedly using one at the Dallas airport when the computer crashed. He was stuck inside the room for six hours. **F**

FW: "Check out this new bathroom!"

AERIAL FOR BROADBAND INTERNET CONNECTION

COMPUTER PLASMA SCREEN

WATERPROOF COMPUTER KEYBOARD

FLAT SCREEN SWIVELS OUT

WIRELESS KEYBOARD CAN BE USED ON LAP

COMPUTER WITH 6 CHANNEL SURROUND SOUND

Don't believe everything you read on the Internet. **≪**

DEAD ENDS

DEATH BY POTATO

A boy jammed a potato up the exhaust pipe of his teacher's car. He waited in the bushes to see what would happen. The teacher drove off—but the hot potato shot out and hit the boy smack between the eyes. **F**

People who pass on **urban myths** like to tell stories about **villains** who come to a messy end. If someone in an urban myth gets what he or she deserves, we can usually smile, however horrible the ending is. **Bizarre** deaths are only interesting when we are not involved!

THE CURSE OF THE CAR

A man named Jones bought his dream car on October 17, 1989. It was a fancy red Porsche. He drove off to watch a baseball game in California. During that historic game, an earthquake hit the city of San Francisco. The game was called off as people ran for their lives.

Careful when you play a practical joke—it could backfire!

SHOCK AND HORROR

Jones ran from the stadium with everyone else and swore. Not only was the game canceled, but a thief had also stolen his new Porsche. On top of all this, everything was at a standstill because of the earthquake.

The car was missing for a few days, since the police were busy dealing with all the problems caused by the earthquake. At last they found the red Porsche. It was under the collapsed Nimitz Freeway. And the thief was still in it. He had died trying to escape in the car he had stolen.

Although this story spread around the world very quickly in 1989, there was no truth in it. Ⓕ

The thief in this **myth** picked the wrong day to steal a car.

DEATH BY RAT LOOK-ALIKE

There is an urban myth that rats come up from the sewers into people's houses. A man named Charles had a terrible fear of rats. He went into the bathroom, where his wife had left her wig beside the sink. The shock of believing that it was a huge rat gave him a heart attack. Ⓣ

This really happened in France in 1988!

BACK TO FRONT

A biker wore his jacket backward to stop the cold from getting through a gap in the zipper. When he crashed and fell off his bike, a passer-by thought the crash had made the biker's head twist around. He tried to turn the head back and broke the biker's neck. (F)

This is just a **myth**—but you should never move an injured person. ⌄⌄

None of these poor men deserved to have such bad things happen to them.

THE UNLUCKY HUSBAND

A man needed to climb onto his roof to adjust the television antenna. He tied a rope around himself for extra safety. He fixed the other end of the rope to the bumper of his car on the other side of the house. But he did not tell his wife what he was doing before he climbed onto the roof. Mistake.

His wife needed to dash to the store and decided to take the car. She drove off, pulled her husband from the roof, and dragged him all the way there. (F)

scuba diver   diver who uses breathing equipment and oxygen in order to breath underwater

FRIED ON THE ICE

A man went ice fishing in Canada. He drove his jeep onto a frozen lake and let his dog out. The man found a place to cut a hole in the ice for his fishing line. The ice was so thick that he could not cut through, and so he decided to cheat. He got a stick of dynamite, lit the fuse, and threw it across the ice. The dog barked and ran after it. The dog was well trained, so it picked up the dynamite and ran back to his master, who screamed before diving for cover in his jeep. This scared the dog, so it hid . . . under the jeep. Boom!

All dog lovers will be glad this is false. Ⓕ

This do-it-yourself safety tip did not go as planned. ⌄⌄

COOKED IN A WET SUIT

After a forest fire, a dead **scuba diver** was found in the ashes. He had not died from burns, but from a fall. It seems he had come from the ocean. Firefighters had used helicopters to scoop up ocean water to drop on the fire. They had scooped up the diver, too. Ⓕ

41

SHRINK-WRAP

In the 1970s, it was the **craze** to wear jeans very tight. A girl bought the latest shrink-to-fit jeans for a perfect skintight fit. She squeezed them on and then sat in the bathtub so they would soak and shrink. The crushing force of the jeans killed her. (F)

This could only happen in an urban myth. >>

DON'T TRY THIS AT HOME

Police often come across mysterious deaths and have to figure out what happened. When a dead body is found in a house, it could be the start of yet another **urban myth** . . . .

KITCHEN MYSTERY

A 39-year-old man **crammed** far too many clothes into his washing machine. Since they would not fit, he climbed on top of the washer to force the clothes inside. That was when he kicked the machine's "on" button by mistake. The washing machine filled with water and began to turn. He lost his balance, and both feet went down into the machine, where they got stuck.

cram   to force something into a small space

IN A SPIN

As the machine started its wash cycle, the man began thrashing around. Suddenly, the machine stopped. His head banged against a shelf, knocking over a bottle of bleach. It poured over his face, blinding him and splashing in his mouth. At this point the washing machine flew into its high-speed spin cycle. He spun at 70 miles (110 kilometers) per hour. His head smashed against a steel beam behind the washing machine, killing him.

The police thought a killer had poisoned the man with bleach, bashed him on the head, and then tried to hide the body in the washing machine. They arrested his wife for murder! Ⓕ

CANADA IN THE FALL

A lawyer in a Toronto skyscraper was showing some students how tough his office windows were. He pushed hard against the glass to show its strength, but he crashed through the window. He plunged 24 floors to his death on the street below. Ⓣ

A Toronto skyscraper is the scene of this modern **myth**.

CLASSIC MIXTURE

POP ROCKS

Pop Rocks were candy that popped and fizzed in the mouth. They were taken off the market in the 1980s after a court case. A boy ate six bags of Pop Rocks washed down by a can of soda. His stomach exploded.

A great story, but you can still buy Pop Rocks and they are safe! **F**

Urban **myths** about food are some of the old favorites. Because we cannot see how our food is prepared, it is easy to imagine these are true.

RODENT TAKE-OUT

A couple went to the local take-out restaurant and bought fried chicken with fries. When they got home, they turned off the lights, switched on the television, and began to eat. They had nearly finished when they both agreed the chicken had an unusual taste. They turned on the light to look more closely. It looked like there was a piece of string on the plate. But it was a tail. The chicken had really been a fried rat!

Things like this may sometimes happen. **?**

> Perhaps more than just your teeth are at risk if you mix candy and cola! »

WEIRD WORDS   **dissolve**   to melt away when in a liquid
formula   instructions showing how something is made

NICE!

On November 28, 2000, a woman named Katherine bought a box of fried chicken in Virginia. When she got them home, she put them out on plates for her family.

Katherine looked again at one of the chicken pieces. It was not like the others. It had an odd shape. She turned it around and then threw it down on the table. It was a chicken's head. It was deep fried, complete with eyes and a beak.

This is probably based on a true story, but there are many **versions** of it. A lot of people seem to know someone who bought a fast food meal and got more than they wanted.   Ⓣ Ⓠ

COLA MYTHS

- It became fizzy by accident when a factory worker dropped soda into a vat.
- If you leave a tooth in cola overnight it will totally **dissolve**.
- Only two people at Coca-Cola know the secret **formula**. They each only know half in case one is kidnapped.

All of these **rumors** are false.   Ⓕ

Some restaurants do not like to waste anything!

---

version   another form of the same story

One type of cactus is home to a beetle that is put in your strawberry milkshake. Red food coloring is made from ground-up South American beetles. It is called cochineal and carmine.

Just another gross **myth**? Sorry—this one is really true! Ⓣ

CACTUS TALES

You cannot beat good stories about plants that fight back. And they could be true.

DESERTED IN THE DESERT

In the Arizona desert there are huge cacti as big as trees. Some are hundreds of years old, and they are protected by law. But one cowboy did not follow the law. He was out with his shotgun, and he wanted to shoot at cacti. He stood close to a giant old cactus and blasted a few holes in its trunk. A great branch gave way and fell right on top of him. It crushed him flat and stabbed him with hundreds of spikes. Alone and unable to crawl away, he died from his wounds. Ⓣ

These cochineal beetles really are added to the food you eat!

This cactus fought back.

Why are peole so scared of tarantulas? **‹‹**

THE TRUTH ABOUT TARANTULAS

There must be more **urban myths** about tarantulas than any other spider. People think that tarantulas are violent and have a deadly bite. Ⓕ

They are actually very shy and do not attack unless **provoked.** Their bites do not cause much harm to humans.

TAKE COVER

A woman always brought back something new for her house when she went away. On one vacation to a very warm country, she brought back a large, rare cactus in a huge pot. It looked greatin her hallway, so she asked some friends over to show them.

During her friends' visit, there was a storm and the lights went off.

Candles and flashlights came out. Suddenly someone screamed, "Look! The cactus is moving. It's alive!"

Everyone ran out and called the police. A cactus expert came to take a close look. Hundreds of poisonous baby spiders were crawling out of the cactus, on the march for food. Ⓕ

YOU CAN'T BEAT A GOOD TUNE

A music student had to write a tune for his homework. He went to the library and found something written by his professor. He copied it out backward, note for note, and turned it in. It came back with the comment, "This is 'I'm Dreaming of a White Christmas.'" **F**

Even the teacher had cheated in the past.

CLASSIC MUSIC

Many **urban myths** are pure **fiction.** We still like to believe they could happen. Some of the funny ones are set in public places where people are supposed to behave properly. But the fun starts when something goes very wrong.

THE CRAZY TROMBONIST

An orchestra was playing a piece of classical music that had guns firing at the end. A trombonist lit a firework and put it down his trombone to make the concert more exciting. He wanted to make a sound like a canon going off.

conductor   person standing in front of an orchestra who leads the musicians

The firework shot out from the front of the trombone. It flew into the **conductor,** throwing him backward off the stage.

GRAND FINALE

The conductor fell onto the front row of the audience. The chairs knocked into the seats behind. Seats fell backward row-by-row, as the audience went down like a row of dominoes. Legs waved in the air as people fell. Meanwhile, a jet of hot gas shot through the trombone's mouthpiece and slammed into the trombonist's face. The bang burned his lips and knocked him out.

Later, from his hospital bed, he said through his bandages, "I thought the end of my trombone would shield me from the explosion. I wanted the concert to end with a bang." It did that, all right.

F

> A concert that went off with a bang. ❝

FRONT TO BACK

John Lennon wrote a song called "Because." It was on the Beatles' album *Abbey Road.* But people said if they played it backward, it was another tune. It sounded like a well-known piano piece by Beethoven, *The Moonlight Sonata.* F

It is not quite the same tune.

FAULTY GOODS

People often say:

- Out of every 100 parachutes, the factory gets three twisted.
- Cars built on Friday afternoons have a 90 percent chance of having faulty brakes.
- Some cheap frozen dinners have human fingernails inside.

They are just more classic **myths!** (F)

TRUE CLASSIC—THAT IS FALSE!

There are hundreds of **urban myths** going around all the time. They are always changing and turning up with new twists. No collection of urban myths would be complete without this famous horror story. Everyone knows it is false, but we still like to feel an icy shiver when we hear it told. This is one **version.**

THE HOOK

A young couple sat in a car parked on Lovers Lane. The girl was **nervous** after the radio reported that a crazy killer was on the loose. He was called "the Hook" because one of his hands was missing and he wore a hook in its place.

Parachutists hope this urban myth are false. ❯❯

JUST IN TIME

The girl would not stop talking about "the Hook," with his hood and the deadly weapon on the end of his arm. The boy got fed up and decided to drive her home. He lost his temper and drove off really fast. He did not say a word on the way home. When they arrived at the girl's house, he got out of the car and went around to open her door. On the door, there was a bloody hook hanging from the handle.

This story may be false, but it is based on real events—like the Lovers Lane murders that happened in Texarkana, Texas, in 1946. ⒡

"The Hook" has all the ingredients of a great urban myth. It is scary. It has a great twist. And it could happen to anyone.

THE SCORE

From about 75 urban myths in this book, this chart shows how the score stands:

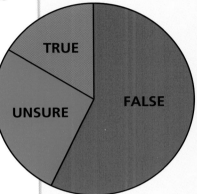

It may not tell us a lot about urban myths other than: *You can never really be sure.*

51

FIND OUT MORE

WEBSITES

AMERICAN FOLKLORE
Includes myths, tall tales, and ghost stories from across the United States.
americanfolklore.net

SPIDER MYTHS
Myths about all types of spiders.
spiders.ucr.edu

BOOKS
Brinkerhoff, Shirley. *Contemporary Folklore.* Broomall, Penn.: Mason Crest, 2002.

Brunvand, Jan Harold. *Too Good to Be True: The Colossal Book of Urban Legends.* New York: W.W. Norton, 2003.

Holf, David and Bill Mooney. *Spiders in the Hairdo: Modern Urban Legends.* Little Rock: August House, 1999.

WORLD WIDE WEB
If you want to find out more about urban myths, you can search the Internet using keywords such as these:
- urban + legends (or "myths")
- amazing stories

You can also find your own keywords by using words from this book. The search tips opposite will help you find the most useful websites.

SEARCH TIPS

There are billions of pages on the Internet, so it can be difficult to find exactly what you are looking for. For example, if you just type in "water" on a search engine such as Google, you will get a list of more than 80 million web pages. These search skills will help you find useful websites more quickly:

- Know exactly what you want to find out about first.
- Use simple keywords instead of whole sentences.
- Use two to six keywords in a search, putting the most important words first.
- Be precise—only use names of people, places, or things.
- If you want to find words that go together, put quote marks around them—for example, "urban myth" or "tarantula myths."
- Use the advanced section of your search engine.

WHERE TO LOOK

SEARCH ENGINE

A search engine looks through the entire Web and lists all the sites that match the keywords. It can give thousands of links, but the best matches are at the top of the list. Try searching with **google.com.**

SEARCH DIRECTORY

A search directory is more like a library of websites. You can search by keyword or subject and browse through the different sites as you would look through books on a library shelf. A good example is **yahooligans.com.**

GLOSSARY

absurd   crazy or ridiculous

ambush   to attack by surprise

awkward   embarrassed and unsure of oneself

bizarre   very strange or weird

blunder   mistake

cashier   person who works at a cash register or a bank

cleaver   knife with a heavy, wide blade

conductor   person standing in front of an orchestra who leads the musicians

cram   to force something into a small space

craze   passing fad or fashion

culprit   guilty person

defrost   to remove frost or ice from something

dissolve   to melt away when in a liquid

disturb   to interrupt someone's rest

embarrass   to cause someone to feel awkward and ashamed

evidence   information to help prove if something is true

far-fetched   sounding too strange to be true

fiction   story made up from the imagination

formula   instructions showing how something is made. It is similar to a recipe.

gadget   small electronic or mechanical device

grisly   causing horror and disgust

horrified   shocked and fearful, or disgusted

intruder   someone who breaks into another person's property

last respects   final farewell to someone who has died

last rites   final prayers for someone about to die

legend   story based on a grain of truth

lie detector   machine that records a person's reactions during questioning. It is used to tell if a person is telling the truth.

lurk   to wait around, ready to strike

myth   made-up tale, told over the years and passed down

nervous   easily scared

outback   wild country in Australia, miles from any towns

pacemaker   electronic device for helping to steady the heartbeat

Pekingese   breed of small dog with long hair and a snub nose

prey victim to be killed or eaten

provoke to annoy or to stir into action

remote faraway place in the middle of nowhere

reptiles group of cold-blooded animals, such as snakes, lizards, and crocodiles

rice paddy flooded field in which rice is grown

rumor story based on gossip

scuba diver diver who uses special equipment and oxygen in order to breathe underwater

scrub thorny bushes and tufts of grass

sinister appearing to be harmful or evil

suction gripping from the removal of air, causing a vacuum

survive to stay alive despite dangers

tall tale story that is very silly and hard to believe

talons claws of a bird of prey

technology use of machines and equipment for doing tasks

thrive to grow in strength and health

trade buying and selling goods

undertaker someone who arranges funerals

urban myth modern popular story that could be true but probably is not

vanish to disappear

version another form of the same story

villain "bad guy" in a story

ward section of a hospital for certain kinds of patients

INDEX